From the Heavens to my Hands

A Collection of Poems
Sarah Levine

Published by JGU Press, 2023

Cover illustration & book design
by Susannah Levin

From the Heavens to My Hands

ISBN: 979-8-218-22939-9
First Edition — June 2023

Copyright © 2023 by JGU Press

Jewish Girls Unite
12 Thompson Hill Rd
Rensselaer NY, 12144
www.JewishGirlsUnite.com

Printed in the USA

Dedication

This book is dedicated to my mother. She taught me everything I know about connection and love. I grew up as a child with confidence and self esteem because I would look into her eyes and see overflowing pride. Without her love I would not have written this book, I would not be living such a beautiful and full life.

Connection is the foundation and I am so grateful to have gotten that. "The living shall take to heart." I will continue her legacy of empathy and kindness. This book being one way to express that.

Thank you, Mommy.

Author's Note

I never liked introductions I usually skip them but I need to write my own. So here it is. My book is raw and real. It is a journey that I am still going through. I wanted to publish this book before I got out of my teenage years because I want this book to feel relatable to teenagers. This book is my heart and soul. This book is a collection of thoughts I picked up in the short amount of years I have been on this earth. I will probably look back at this book and feel embarrassed by it. But that's part of the journey.

Embrace it.

Hold it, you are the only one who can write your story. Whether it is through music, art, dance, or your participation in this world. There are times I feel I want to be someone else or live some other life. But I would never have written this if I had a different life. So although it sucks sometimes it also is really great. Your life is yours and I hope these poems inspire you to figure out how to make your life your own. How to create a home within yourself.

Acknowledgments

To my Mother:

For bringing me into this world and shaping the way I act in it.

To my Father:

For your support, silent, or noticable. I know you want the best for me no matter what.

To my brother Mendel:

For listening to my "cheesy poems" yet still calling them good. I appreciate all your feedback and advice.

To my other Brothers:

For being in my life. Giving me rides or $5 when I need it.

To my Uncle:

You agreed to help me and gave me pep talks.

For my Bnos Chomesh High School principal, Mrs Gorkin:

You told me I should write this, thank you for always believing in me.

To my friend Teshuva:

Thanks for making me read poems at slams and commenting on the lines you liked. Ahhhhh!

To my teachers:

Thank you for your support and advice.

To the random people I meet:

Thank you for listening to my poetry.

Thank you Nechama Laber, founder of the JGU Press, for making my dream come true. You made this a top priority in your busy life and I am so appreciative of that. Thank you for coordinating with your team of designers and editors. Thank you for your encouragement and belief in me throughout this process.

To Tzipporah Prottas, editor. Thank you for your incredible work to make this happen.

Thank you, Susannah Levin, who took my ideas and made them into a beautiful book cover. Thank you for for laying out the pages of the book and helping me divide the sections.

To G-d:
I literally would not exist without You. Thank You for sustaining me to this moment, and giving me the talents I have so I can spread them to the world.

About Sarah Levine:

Sarah is 20 years old. She is currently learning in Beis Chaya Mushka Seminary in Montreal. She began journaling when she was just twelve years old. (She has about 10 notebooks since then) Writing is her release and her joy. She also really loves babies, spending time in nature and hanging out with animals. She would love to get to know you! So please do reach out at heavenstomyhands@gmail.com.

Table of Contents

Part I

"Those who sow with
tears will reap with song"

הזערים בדמעה ברינה יקצורו

Tehillim 125:5

A Place I Wish I Knew

Home
A place I wish I knew
A place I keep finding, and losing
And finding again.
I'm unsure what it means,
Does it mean love?
Does it mean comfort?
These I feel sporadically,
Unpredictably.
So, perhaps my home is in many places?
But home, I thought to mean one place—
I feel love and comfort and I wonder is this home?
But where do I go when these feelings ebb and flow?
I can't go back to what life should have been.
Right now it doesn't look like I can begin.
So I close my eyes
I imagine a home.

A home filled with love and laughter,
And perhaps some chaos.
I imagine this home to be mine.

My Little Island

My heart fills with longing,
My throat dry from thirst,
Alone on my little island.
A boat sails nearby trying to reach me—
But then before anyone comes, the boat sails away.
Occasionally, the boat returns.
The passengers throw me some food,
Some clothes,
Some water, perhaps.
But nobody comes to get me.
There are too many important things to attend to
On the boat.
They think they're doing a great thing for me—
"We're giving you food, clothes,
Some money here and there.
You've got nothing to worry about."
But nobody realizes that I want to get off my little island,
That I want to be held in their arms and
   have my tears wiped away.
I want them to find
Me important enough to get off the boat.
They tell me I can swim to them,
I try, but my arms get too weak to keep moving.

So, before I sink,

I get back to my little island.

Nobody even realized I was sinking.

And so, time after time—

I am tired.

Tired of trying to get someone to do something,

But I'm too tired as well to do it myself.

Stranger in the Mirror

I feel I will never know who I am

Because truly I know who I am

But I am confused

Because I do not feel what I think is me

And that causes my heart to pump out if its chest

My throat to form a lump,

Fear—

I am filled with fear

Because the unknown is terrifying

And not knowing yourself

Is worse

Because you can never run away from yourself

Why do I feel so different

All the time?

Why can't I just look into a mirror

And say, "Yeah, that's me"?

Why do I even feel weird being called by my name

Or introducing myself?

Sometimes I feel as if I am watching myself

And sometimes, I feel as if I am a different version
   of what I think I am

I'm always confused

Afraid of my own reflection

In an attempt to ground myself

I tell myself my name, my age, the school I go to

Yes, this is my room

But those words feel foreign in my mind

   and on my tongue

I try to place myself where I know I am

But it doesn't fit

My head spins the world looks strange

I am confused

I am afraid

And somehow I know that,

Even though I don't know my own reflection.

G-d, How Can I Trust You?

G-d how can I trust you?
I have been hungry and cold,
I have been lonely and afraid,
I have been abandoned,
By You.
You took my safety away
And now I go about this world as if in the dark,
Not seeing the next step in front of me—
And I am afraid!
Yet they all say to trust You,
You whom I cannot fathom?
You Whom I cannot see?
You Whom is responsible for it all?
Each creature is here at your mercy!
And as much as I don't know how I can trust you
I also know I can't not trust you
For how can I not?
When I see the pure smile of a child,
When I hear the leaves rustling in the wind,
Feel the sun on my skin—
The powerful sun, which if too close can return me to nothing-
     ness,
If too far this world would be too cold to inhabit.

This world is perfection.

This world is unfathomable.

This world,

Is You.

And so although I cannot see the next step,

    I know it is all there for me.

Although I no longer have the one who made me feel safe

I know if You care for each leaf and each rock and each star

And all are in its place.

Then, G-d I know you will put me in mine.

I am at this moment where You have put me.

I trust You G-d.

For there is none else to put my trust in.

Young

I was so young
Convinced I could handle it all
But I didn't know what I was even trying to handle
I look back at younger me
I wish I could go back in time and comfort her
Hold her, bring her dinner,
Tell her she doesn't need to be the one to hold it all together.
But I know she would refute me
She would tell me,
"If I don't, nobody else will"
And I cannot help but agree,
But to nod my head
Perhaps with tears in my eyes
That I will try hard to hide, because
I know how much you hate when people cry.
You still hate when people cry.
I can't go back and comfort you,
Because nothing anyone told you then helped you either
But I want to go back and protect you
As I hold babies now I think of you,
My younger self
And how you so badly wanted someone to just hold you
You still do.

You are inside me, constantly looking,

Desperately

For someone who could be your mother

But you are a little bird that fell out of the nest

You ask the kitten, the hen and even the cow

But no, they are not your mother

And as the little bird said, "I want to go home, and I want my

    mother!"

But unlike the little bird

You still can't find your mother,

Or your home.

I am here to tell you

Although you feel so abandoned and alone

I will never forget you

I will never leave you

I will hold you

And I honor all you have done

because I would not be who I am without you.

A Hug

A hug
That feeling of—
It doesn't matter to me where you have been,
What you have done.
I feel comfortable enough
To have my body against yours.
I trust you enough
To bury my head in your shoulders.
To seek comfort from your tight embrace.
As if to say that everything's ok.
I can almost feel your heart against mine,
Your steady beat slowing my rapid one.
Or, perhaps the opposite?
Or, both our hearts are beating too fast,
    but they are comforted by the presence of another.
To feel the warmth,
To feel your chest going in and out as you breathe,
Reminding me to breathe.
I relax,
Slowly.

Not realizing I was even tense before.

And although I wiggle out of the embrace,

I don't really want to.

If you take your arms out from around me,

I am suddenly aware of how cold the world feels.

But I am still left warm.

Costume

When people neglect to put on their uniforms
I put on a cloak of responsibility.
Responsibility that should not belong to me.
I am drowning in tasks which are too much for me,
Tripping in clothes far too big on me.
A baby in her mothers shoes,
I cannot go far without falling.
As I try to keep these garments from getting lost,
My own start to slip away.
I want to run through a forest of trees and brooks
Perhaps the clothes will get caught in the bushes,
Tear them from my own small body.
Perhaps the brook will take the cloak with its current,
I will watch as it swirls away until it is gone from sight.
And then,
I will be free.
Free to put on a costume, not just some uniform.
Or perhaps I was wearing a costume all this time?
The illusion of control.
I am free.
 I just have to realize

G-d is holding up the world for me
Even though I can't see
For He wears cloaks to conceal His light.
But if I were to take off my costume
    perhaps He would take off his own
And show me that I have nothing to fear.

Run

He tells me to take what I have and run with it
Run?
How can I run when I don't know where I'm going?
When the only thing I see in front of me is darkness
And I look behind
But all I see are the things I wish I had
I look down
The ground
That my feet are standing on
Is a less than ideal life
A life filled with grief
And disappointment
Yet a life filled with love
Filled with laughter
Filled with people who care
My heart starts pumping faster
My feet ready to run
Ready to leave behind all I wish I had
I don't know where I will end up
But I know along the way there will be something
    to add to my foundation
Something for my feet to stand on
At times

The path looks blurry
My eyes filled with tears
At times I look back and can't move forward
And at times it feels exhilarating
Exciting
I feel the passion pumping blood into my legs
I'm running faster and further
And then I fall
And sometimes
There's no one there to pick me up
No one there
But my own two feet
And I look down at them
And see the key to my life
Enough waiting around for someone to be something
    to me that I want them to be
And just allow them to be part of my journey
Even if they won't always be there for me
G-d, I'm told I can always turn to You
You're the one Who did this all to me
And also the one Who breathes life into me
Who created my feet to run
My eyes to see

My heart to feel

Nobody is consistent

Nobody is forever

And King David's words come to mind

"My mother and father have abandoned me,

   but G-d has taken me in"*

King David?

Did you feel the same as me?

Did you have to use your feet to run

Even when you couldn't see the path in front of you?

When everyone you cared about and

   those who should have cared for you rejected you

And yet you fought and won battles

You were a mighty king

You wrote,

Turned your pain into meaning.

King David

I am not you

But I have feet too,

Feet that can run—

Run with what I have.

*Tehillim 27:10

In and Out

I breathe
In and out
Just like the ocean
The waves retreating and returning eternally from the shore
My feet sink into the sand
The sun caresses me
I breathe, in and out
Just like the ocean.
My heart constricts
I am now fighting the
waves that threaten to drown me
My mind is racing, my body us shaking
I can't breathe because if I do, these waters will overtake me.
I struggle to free myself,
But my mistakes become weights
Dragging me down
"You can't win," they tell me
"You never succeeded before," they lie to me
But somehow,
I know that I want to breathe again!
To feel my feet sink into the sand,
The sun caressing me—
And so, with strength I didn't know I had

I kick off the weights.

I know these waters can't drown me

They're only there to lift me higher

And so, I surface.

My head out of the water,

I surface.

I am brought to land

Exhausted.

Afraid of the beautiful waves that just threatened to drown me

But I know that I want to breathe again

So, I stand

I breathe, in and out

I watch as the waves return and retreat eternally from the
    shore.

My feet sink into the sand,

The sun caresses me

I breathe in and out

Just like the ocean.

Part II

"Hashem is with me, I shall not fear"
ה׳ לי ולא אירא אדון עולם

Your World is Shaking at Its Core

Your world is shaking at its core.

Your beliefs feel so untrue.

Everything you ever thought is brought to court.

People you thought you knew,

You no longer do.

The things you thought were so true

Now feel so unreal.

You thought you knew yourself,

And realized you had but very little clues...

The world is shaking at its core

All inside you,

Your mind churns,

Your heart burns.

What now am I to do

If this all isn't true?

Or even worse,

What if it is?

It's not all black and white,

There is wrong,

There is right.

Yet, in right,

There are so many ways.

Yet, none of them

Are wrong.

Your world may not yet, (not ever) feel secure

As you try to find what's true.

But it sure helps when you realize,

The colors of your world

Have many hues.

Pendulum

It seems my choices swing in a pendulum.
I'm never sure which side is right
Because it swings so quick
I can't catch the choices being laid out in front of me.
My mind is in a dance trying to catch the clues
    to what I should do.
My eyes swing
Back and forth.
Hypnotized in uncertainty.
What I think,
Or
What she said?
What I feel,
Or
What in my mind I know is right?
Or
Perhaps what I really feel is right?
And what I'm thinking really is true?
You tell me something,
And then say,
"It's up to you."
Don't tell me anything, if you won't tell me what to do!

So, my head turns foggy as the pendulum swings
Back and forth...
My body is taken over
By the fear
Of failure.
The pendulum
Did its job.
Ridding me of the choice I had,
With its uncertainty.
I close my eyes,
I no longer see the pendulum.
My mind slows,
My breath calms,
I imagine how the choices I make might impact me
And actively choose the one that appears right.
I take a leap of faith,
And believe this will be what's best for me,
And that the Al—Mighty will help me.

Expecting Perfection

I see an empty paper
My heart is too full to know what to put on it.
I am expecting perfection with every word,
Expecting perfection in every move.
But, my life is filled with imperfection.
Expecting clarity,
Yet my mind is being swayed by all opinions.
Confusion is inevitable.
I like to know what's happening,
But uncertainty is impossible to avoid.
It's like walking on rocks in a brook,
But it's so slippery I fall in.
I fall and get wet,
Filled with anger when I wish I can be filled with gratitude.
Trying to do all those things I think I should be able to do.
Thought I could make friends,
But I am left lonely.
My desperation is pushing people away.
I try to be fearless,
But fear is there like a rock in my chest.
Insecurity,
There like a fly buzzing around me.
The sweet feeling of accomplishment

That fills me, too.
The joy of life's goodness,
Of laughter and friends,
Love.
It's there as well.
When I sit by that brook
Yes, the one I have slipped into
Peace fills me.
Just as G-d made nature, so He made me.
And I know I'm never truly alone.
And still I slip,
Into the unknown abyss,
But the water is sometimes less deep than I thought...

There

My mind is loud

My body tense

I just cannot relax

I do do do do

Do all the things I should

I should should should do all the things I do

Check off every box and more

But something is missing

Something but what?

I look toward the goal

And get stuck on all the little things

And sometimes I cannot do what I need to do

    to get to my goal

And so the tasks circle in my mind

Until I am *there*

But once I am *there*

My mind frantically searches for more things to latch on to

And I think I will be good once I am *there*

But *there* keeps moving

Perhaps *there* does not exist

And maybe I should not try to get *there*

Maybe I need to be *Here*

Why does it seem like everyone has it all together,

When I know that everyone feels like they will explode?!

Sometimes, for an unknown reason.

I know everyone has a hard time with things.

So, why do I feel like a failure?

I can laugh at myself,

But inside I'm angry that yet again I didn't succeed.

I still wake up late,

I still go to sleep late.

So, why does it seem like everyone else functions
    better than me?

Why is it fair

That some people are just more relaxed?

Why does it seem that I'm being judged?

Am I making it up?

Or, perhaps it is the truth...

I am so afraid that I will disappoint
    the expectations people have of me.

Afraid that they look at me the way I look at myself.

Expecting so much

That every little fall bruises me so badly.

I know I'm doing my best,

I know that everyone has a hard time.
So, why does it seem that time after time,
I am spearing daggers into my own heart?
Why can't I just accept imperfection?
Why am I so afraid of it?
Afraid of messing up my life,
Of messing up someone else's?
Most of all, afraid of this fear…

Pulverize

I want to pulverize my thoughts into tiny pieces
That fly away into the wind and no longer are distinguishable
I want to unravel the circles so tightly binding
　　my legs, my chest, my head
I want to melt my worries in a pot big enough
　　to fit my burdens
Hot enough to force my stubborn muscles to relax
My mind finds no ease
No rest
It finds something to latch on to, however small
And does not let go
I so envy the smile I put on everyday
It's not fake
Yet still does not quite penetrate
I so envy people who can take vacations
No matter where I am
My thoughts pulverize my peace
I am happy
Just still so anxious
I like my mind
But I feel like my mind doesn't like me
Doesn't want me to relax
It's constantly fighting a battle

That nobody sees

Sometimes even me

It's fighting a battle it doesn't need to fight

But it doesn't care how many times I tell it that

My mind is trying to protect me

But I am trying to relax

How many times must I be reminded of the things
    I can't take care of right now?

How many times must I be reminded of the to—do list
    as I am completing it?

How many times must I be reminded of the appointment
    I already made

And did I actually make it?

Do I remember the right time?

Does my mind not trust me?

I guess it doesn't

But I keep trying to prove that I can do this

But the amount of checked—off items doesn't make me feel
    any better

So, maybe I should stop trying

But that won't help either

I'm trying so hard

To be functional

I am functioning

But my mind won't let me rest

I'm so done

I'm trying to prove myself

But nothing is working

And I just want to pulverize my thoughts

And melt my worries

And all I will be left with

Is me

In my essence

Foreboding is familiar

Foreboding is familiar
And still
Unsettling
In the back of my mind a worry always nags me
What if?
What if?
What if?
And I distract if and think I got rid of it until
Something makes me withdraw into those spiraling thoughts
And those feelings of fear
And I no longer let myself feel joy
Because anything can happen
And things can get ruined
And my life I worked so hard to put back together can again
  break
But was it ever really together?
One after the other after the other
Little things
Big things
When did everything start feeling like an emergency?
And yet it feels comfortingly familiar
And something is making me hold on
Making me think that I need to worry about this

That this could be serious

That maybe I should listen to my instinct

But is it my instict or anxiety?

Are my feeling true or just my imagination gone horribly wild?

"Grief kid, why do you always think the worst?

Because the worst has happened."

And I'm beginning to think this feeling
    will follow me wherever I go

Sometimes I wont feel it

And sometimes it will come out of the bed and scare me
    in the middle of the night

And I can't tell it that it's just a monster

Because sometimes it's right

But there's nothing I can do anyways

The monster is not the thought

It's the control the thought has over me

It gets bigger and bigger and bigger

As I worry and worry and worry

And I wish it was as simple as climbing on my mother's bed
    and spraying the monsters with our imaginary spray

The pink spray getting rid of the girl monsters

The blue ones getting rid of the boy monsters

But these thought don't get scared away

I get scared away by the thoughts
And so now it's all reversed
And I can't climb on my mother's bed no matter how much I
    want to.
So I look at the monster in the face
And tell it
"I don't need you"
I look at the monster in the face and discover within it
A scared little girl
And I tell her "G-d is protecting you"
And still she flails and screams
Still she gets larger as the night darkens
Still she scares me
And perhaps this is a struggle I will always have
But not a struggle I will succumb to

Part III

"Words that come from the heart
enter the heart"

Hidden growth

In the winter, barely anything blooms.
The wind and snow,
Rain and cold
Wet the earth
So that in a few months time,
Things will grow.
But in the moment,
It is dark,
It is cold,
In moments like that—
You can't expect yourself to blossom.
It will come after.
Growth does not always mean to bloom,
Sometimes it means to wait.
In those moments, your seeds are below the earth.
Growing roots into the soil,
Strength invisible to the human eye.
Does a farmer hate the crops that won't grow
   when they are not yet ready?
Be kind,
It takes
time.

Too young

She tries to push the buttons
Refutes every answer we give her
She doesn't realize that she has already stumped us
That nobody can really answer her question
I hear her voice laced with pain
Her eyes glazed in hopelessness
That she tries to disguise as defiance
"What if nobody understands and I have nobody to talk to?"
Someone tells her to reach out.
"But what if they're too far away?"
"Reach further."
"What if my arms are too short?"
"Just like the clouds cover the sun, but we know it is always
    there—
there are people who will always be there, even if you don't
    see."
Weak arguments
This girl has been shown again and again
    that nobody understands her.
When people tell her things like,
"You're too young for problems."
When people say,
 "I'm always here for you"

But she sends texts and nobody answers,
And she is realizing now that adults are not perfect.
To ask her to see the light, to reach out,
You're adding expectations on to her
She is not too young for problems—
But she may be too young to solve them.
She may be too young to ask for help.
Because how can you ask for help
   when you don't even know where to start?
When you have thoughts and feelings you can't explain
And don't understand yourself?
I want to tell you it gets better,
But I know "better" feels impossible.
I want to tell you how loved you are,
But I know you don't feel it, even if you know it.
I want to promise to always be here for you,
But I can't always be there when you need me.
I can't say I understand you,
Because even if we would have gone through the same thing,
I am not you.
So I open my mouth and say,
"No matter what I tell you, it will not help
   until you understand and believe it yourself"

And I see a flicker of hope in her eyes—
Oh.
Someone gets it.
In them, I see who I was,
And only now do I see how things can get better.
Change doesn't feel impossible.
Their seeds are planting roots into the soil.
We won't see them bloom for a while—
They need patience.
And someone who understands that they are growing,
    even if it doesn't look like it

Who can't forgive?

I'm sorry.
What other words can I say
To mend the pain I inflicted?
How can I say that?
If I know,
I wouldn't forgive you,
If what I had done to you
You have done to me.
Is my "I'm sorry"
Worth it?
Even if I mean it?
Perhaps it is I
Who can't forgive.
But how can I not forgive,
When I know
How much regret I feel
When I say those two simple words?
When I know that whatever I did,
I never wanted to hurt you?
At least not for real,
And not for long.
When I say sorry,
I mean it.

And now,

I must mean it to myself.

Pressure to be

I'm overwhelmed
By my mind that just won't let me be
Constantly
Constantly
Turning everyday things into huge mountains
But then again maybe they are huge mountains
But I just hate feeling like this
I'm frustrated
Tired of this
Of it all
Pressure
To be something to someone
Something to myself
Pressure to perform
And I can't take a break
Because it is all on me
And who will take care of it, if not I?
Who will be for me, if I am not for myself?
But I want someone to be for me
If not now, when?
But not everything happens now
I have to wait,
I have to be patient,

I have to...
So many 'I have to's
So many obligations
Rules
Structures
So, how can I relax,
When the whole world just won't
Slow down?
Just won't lessen its grip
Because I cannot lessen my grip.
If I do,
Then who will tighten it when it needs to be?
But who says my grip needs to be so tight?

Pedestal

Hi,
I just met you
In my eyes, you are on a pedestal.
Greater than I,
Immune to mistakes,
Immune to expressing emotions in unhealthy ways.
I just met you,
Forgive me.
I'm just trying to find perfection.
Trying to find someone to hold on to.
Oh,
It's not you?
Hmmm… Well, this is awkward…
My dreams shattered to the ground again and again.
When those I thought would be there for me
    cry on my shoulder.
When those I thought were the kindest, most sensitive people
Say insensitive things.
When someone I thought I could hang out with says,
"No."

My expectations of you are high
I know.
I'm just trying to find someone to hold on to
Oh
It's not you, either?

Friends

I felt warm inside as we laughed,

As we talked about our dreams.

I keep wishing for a friend,

But it seems my wish was causing a rift in all those that may

   have been my friends.

Craving for something,

Trying to get it...

Afraid she won't reciprocate.

But connection comes naturally,

I can't force it.

It comes with questions I'm too afraid to ask.

It comes with knowing when to do what,

And not always do I know...

It comes with accepting that relationships

   are fluid and confusing.

That perhaps there is someone she is friends with,

   and I'm not that person.

It feels as though everyone else knows

Something I don't…

I have friends, just not the way the people around me

   have them.

I feel left out

I will myself to just laugh along,
Play card games.
Ask questions I'm too afraid to ask,
Listen
Really listen.
Be a friend,
Just a friend.
Have something special with that one person.
A little joke,
Your relationship logo.
Not every person I meet will be a friend
But I can start conversations
And gain something from everyone.

Snubbed

Belonging feels so far away.
I try starting conversations
Asking questions
Joining in
Yet again and again there is something about me that does not
    fit in
Perhaps I'm just different,
Unrelatable.
Too deep, too confusing.
Do I make people feel uncomfortable?
Anxious?
Do people just skip over me?
Just don't give me a chance to be part of their group?
Am I sharing too much?
But it seems as though that is how the other girl got herself in
I remember complaining in second grade that
    if I wore something it was weird
But suddenly the "queen" wore it and it was cool
And it's not fair
But, do I really want to belong with a group?
Be tied down to what they think is acceptable?
Not knowing which characteristics are mine and
    which are my friends'?

I know myself so well.

Probably because I have nobody hindering that.

But I'm still lonely,

I still feel snubbed,

And it's still unfair that when "the queen" wears it, it's cool

And so, to all those, who people are friendly to,

   but have no friends

Know that you are no less because of it.

Dreamer

I'm a dreamer.

The kind that imagines a reunion and spends 5 minutes just staring at the salt in the grocery aisle, forgetting that I need to pick up the sugar.

I imagine my graduation speech in 9th grade

Being interviewed throughout the world about the epiphany I just had and how it changed the world.

I live more in times that do not exist yet or may not ever happen...

And with this dreaming comes fear.

Fear, because what if these things I really want won't happen?

And I can't accept what is now.

So, I live more in times that do not exist yet or may not ever happen.

But they exist in my imagination and

As my head is filled with graduation speeches

Or reunions with long—lost friends

A smile comes to my face

There is a spring in my step

But then—

BOOM

I have no way of seeing my friend

I don't get that job

And my hopes are crushed

My faith challenged

Does G-d really care?

But foolishly, my crushed spirits don't last too long

I like my hope,

It keeps me alive.

I like my belief—I know there's purpose.

It keeps the spring in my step,

The sparkle in my eyes.

But how long can I keep telling myself lies?

Are they lies?

But should I keep hoping if hope almost always ends
in disappointment?

Should I keep trusting if every time I trust, I am reminded
why I should stop caring?

I am reminded of why it does not help.

There's no way anyone can tell me my prayers will be answered,

Nobody knows.

I want to stop yearning,

But if I never yearn for anything, then what would be exciting?

The joy of anything relies on how much you want it.

And although some dreams get shattered like shards of glass

As life changes.

Sometimes I need to create new dreams

Realistic dreams

Dreams that make me smile,

Add a sparkle to my eyes

A spring in my step

And perhaps I need to live in times that exist now
    and are happening

And maybe there is a plan I don't know about.

Fighting a losing battle

I am fighting a losing battle
Chasing a feeling of content
And I think,
I just need to do this project.
I just need to write this poem.
I just need to read this book.
I just need to relax.
I just need to hang out with friends.
I just need to go to sleep and wake up on time.
Then I will feel accomplished.
So, why is it that whenever I do these things, I still feel
    something is missing?
I can spend an entire day doing things
And still I will feel as if I spent the day in unproductivity.
Feeling like there's something missing,
A void—
That no matter how many actions I do, it does not fill.
I just feel inadequate
I just feel like nothing will ever, ever be good enough.
If I relax, I can't forgive myself for not doing anything.
At the end of a long day
I can't forgive myself for not relaxing.
I feel the need to have that balance.

I look around and see something in someone else I don't have.

I don't work out.

I don't spend time in the park reading.

I don't go out with my friends almost every night.

I didn't have that idea.

I will never be happy,

So long as I chase someone else's happinesses.

I will never feel successful,

So long as I chase an idea of success that does not exist.

And part of my imperfections is my perfectionism

The more I fight it, the smarter it gets—

The bigger it gets.

And so, though I feel the temptation to defend myself

I will not let you convince me,

That I am not doing my best because you are still here…

The rules of confidence

I am well versed in the rules of confidence.
Yet, my feeling of inadequacy don't seem to care that
"I'm doing my best."
She tells me my best isn't good enough.
She doesn't care that "my productivity does
    not define my worthiness."
Inadequacy, she tells me that I'm a failure,
    that I'll never get anything done
She is an expert salesperson,
Selling me lies,
Making them seem like truths.
She convinces me I need these thoughts.
That without them I will not go forward.
Yet, all they do is take up space.
All they do is weigh me down.
I try to shake off the weights.
I try to quiet her incessant chatter.
Yet, the more I try to stamp her out,
The stronger she gets.
She always has something clever to say
To convince me that she's right.
To convince me I'm not good enough.
The more words I give her,

The more fuel is added to her fire.
So, perhaps she does not need words.
Perhaps nothing will convince her otherwise...
"Wrestling with a dirty person just makes you dirty"
So, perhaps I should stop wrestling.

Part IV

"The world is a garden, but not just anyone's garden, it's G-d's garden!"

Sicha of the Rebbe
י' שבט
1972

Beyond

After my mom died, I thought about the future a lot.
But still I had narrow vision
I didn't see beyond my disconsolate feelings.
I didn't see that I could still have a life,
That I could be happy.
Really happy.
I spent my time worrying—
I still do.
Where will I be?
What if I am left alone?
I have nothing to fall back on.
I saw my life as an aftermath of the tragedy I have been
    through.
And lately,
My vision became wider,
My smiles more genuine.
I realized
I have my life in front of me!
I can build upon the shattered dreams
And broken hearts.
I can't fix them.

But, I can gather the splintered shards to create a masterpiece.

Adding it all together, taking what life has taught me—

To create the life I want, the life I dream of.

I'm still scared—

Yet, I see something beyond the fear.

Motherless daughter

Motherless daughters

It's a book I'm reading—

And trying to hide from the other people in my house.

Too many questions—

And with questions come the feelings…

And it makes me realize how lonely I am,

It makes me realize I'm an orphan.

I'm a motherless daughter.

And for some reason, everyone has to know

That there is something missing in my life.

When I am trying to just keep moving,

Keep smiling,

Keep happy,

So, when she asked, "Why are you reading that book?

I answered her.

How long could I keep my mothers death out of my life?

But the girl already knew, as I assumed

And so I smiled. and we changed the subject

But now I feel lonely,

Bereaved.

I'm falling down the pit I work so hard to avoid.

I don't have her arms to be held by,

Or her jokes to laugh at,

Nor do I see the love on her face.

I feel that emptiness.

It won't go away so long as she is, well, away.

She taught me kindness,

Resilience,

Sensitivity,

I carry those in my heart.

Every day she lives through what she taught me.

And so when I hold a door open,

When I get water for someone,

When I listen—

I remember her.

Truly, she will not ever be forgotten

Because even if I don't remember what she said or did,

I can always practice what she taught me.

Someone's mother

As I get older I sometimes worry that people will stop
    helping me
That they will think,
"You're an adult you should take care of this yourself."
And that moment has come many times in many ways.
Because sometimes nobody can help me
And then somebody sends me money
A friend's mother helps me.
I have become the daughter of many mothers
And as the years pass my relationships change
And people come in and out of my life.
But each relationship heals a piece of my heart.
A hug before bed
Soup made for me
I am 19 years old
And I want to be mothered, and there is nothing
    wrong with that.
Nothing will bring back my mother
And none of these people are replacing her,
They are doing what she would do for me.
I truly believe she sees me,
And she prays for me,
That G-d will send the right people when I need them.

To teach me what she could not,

To hold me when she can not,

I feel her love in that hug

I feel her nurture and care in that soup

The soul is everlasting

Love is everlasting

As someone's mother told me in tenth grade,

"It doesn't matter if the love comes from my house
    or from yours,

It is all Hashem's love."

So now I feel held and cared for

I feel serene

Because someone's mother took care of me today.

It's all from Hashem,

And so when I feel that nobody is answering me,

I will remember

This moment and the moments that have brought me
    to this moment.

I am a living miracle.

If I have emerged before

I can emerge again

stronger.

A fire in the midst of a forest

You didn't give me a solution.
There was none that you could give me…
You can't change the people in my life I so desperately wish
    I could change.
You can't give me back my mother.
Yet, somehow,
I felt your heart join mine.
I felt my burden lighten.
I felt a warm blanket cover my shivering body.
Your care, your words
Gave me something to hold on to.
A fire in the midst of the snowy forest,
Something to keep me trudging along the deep snow.
You tell me that I can be a light for others,
That even if I crumble, I will get back up.
You tell me that all those people I want to help will look
    at how I helped myself.
And, perhaps they will trudge through the snow
    to get some warmth,
To create their own,
They will keep going.

So, you tell me to hold the hope for them.

You tell me that sometimes I cannot lift the other person,

  lest I fall.

and so sometimes all I can do is care.

And when I fall,

When I cannot see the hope,

I will remember how much you believe in me.

Masterpiece

I sometimes feel the need to create a masterpiece.

To beautify life through words and rhyme.

To show that the scariest things,

The saddest things

May not be sweetened,

Yet to show there is purpose in the pain.

If it is able to be written, perhaps it is able to be worked through.

Purpose in pain,

A hope in the hopeless—

That is what writing does.

Someone understands you when you thought

    you were the only one,

Validation

That is what writing does.

I understand it one way,

You another,

But when I write—

Perhaps we can understand each other.

The power of pen on paper,

The power of a scribble on a napkin,

Fingers on a keyboard.

G-d gave us everything.

And I am thankful to have the ability to write about it all.

I think of you sometimes

I think of you sometimes
The 12 year old me
The 13,14,15,16,17
Year old me
When life felt impossibly hard
When your vision was narrowed
All you could see was anxiety
All you could see was fear
And grief and sadnes
Your mind wrapped in obsessive thoughts
Never ceasing
And till you were 17 you didn't accept that you were sick.
That OCD was something you had to deal with
And some people told you it might take forever.
And I marvel at your endurance,
Your persistence,
That part in you that never gave up.
That prayed every day to the G-d that scared you
Because somehow you knew that your thoughts
    weren't really true—
Weren't really you.
And sometimes I look back and wish I could have
    taken it all away from you.

But I know you had to go through it
Because it made you into who you are.
You lost yourself to find yourself
And I can't believe I am saying this
But I would never trade it.
Although throughout it all
You just wanted to be someone else.
Someone who could just smile, just laugh, just relax.
But you didn't have to be someone else.
You just had to be you
The real you that was hidden in all those layers of thought
    rituals.
I am not angry at you OCD
You were there to protect me
My world was so confusing
I needed to create a reason for things.
But G-d's plan is bigger then I can understand.
I used to say that with trembling lips and shaking hands.
Now I can say that with a calm heart and steady body.
My OCD comes sometimes as a visitor
But leaves after just a thought…
And now I wish to tell people
Your going to be OK

I wish I can hold them and tell them all there is life
    Beyond your obsessions and compulsions.
I prayed every day to G-d even though He scared me
Even though my OCD made him look terrifying
There was part of me that knew the only thing that could get
    me out was Hashem.
And now I thank Him—
I thank Him that I can smile,
That I can laugh,
That I can think without the obsession coming to me.
And I thank Him
Although it is not easy,
I thank Him that I have been through all that hell.
Because through that,
I have emerged as I am today—
With a smile on my face
And a twinkle in my eye
A twinkle of someone who truly knows what it means to
    emerge victorious.

Joy of beauty

The river's waves crash against the rocks.
I laugh at the pure joy of beauty.
It seems all my problems are drowned in the water.
That it is only me
And G-d.
Only the friend beside me, laughing at my amazement
Because both amazement and laughter are contagious.
Nothing matters besides this moment.
All I can see in front of me is the sea and sky.
Feel the cool winds,
Smell the freshness.
My smile gets bigger,
My laugh happier,
Who knew all I needed was the river?
It's amazing how such physicality can make you
    feel so spiritual,
How water and rocks can make you feel G-d.
My breath is almost taken away.
I don't care what I say or how I look.
"THIS IS LIFE ITSELF!"
I get so caught up in what I want,
What I wish I can have,
What I went through...

I get so caught up, I forget the world is beautiful
    even if it's also terrible.
The river doesn't discriminate,
Anyone can enjoy its beauty.
No matter who you are, and what you've been through.
Nature,
The great equalizer,
Beckons for you to enjoy it.
To feel belonging amongst the grass and trees
Along the rocks and waves,
To silently watch deer and geese
And marvel at their beauty—
Marvel at their Creator.

A writer

To be a writer—
Is to be an observer,
a listener.
To be a thinker.
To see the beauty in things most others would not notice.
To walk slowly down a path you have walked down
   so many times before
And notice
The funny license plate,
The fireflies,
The people
And how they talk to each other.
To hear the sentence fragments
And wonder what they are talking about.
To try and grasp the feeling behind those words.
To notice a car park so skillfully
And then see a father coming out with his two sons
To feel the love between them.
The feeling they probably don't notice.
Because it's always there.
To be a writer,
Is to notice.
What has always been there

To cause beautiful feelings out of everyday things.
A writer is not just a person
Who can so wonderfully describe the setting sun
Or the sparkling stars
To be a writer
Is to describe walking down the same path
In the concrete jungle,
As you have many times before,
And make it sound just as beautiful,
Because it is.

Create it?

They tell me to create a home inside myself
To belong to myself
But G-d didn't make us like that
He made us in a way that we are reliant upon each other
And when people that you should be reliant upun for a home
For belonging
Are not reliable
Then what?
Oh create it myself?
Do you even know what that means?
I guess not because nobody ever told me how
What even is a home?
What even is belonging?
To me a home is a place you can always go back to
But when you don't have that, then what?
You can't create that because life is so unpredictable
Belonging
To me that means someone putting her arm
  around my shoulder
She saves me a seat
She goes places with me
And that feeling has been shattered again and again

When I was pushed out of the kiddie pool
When she says, "oh this is someone's seat"
And it's never mine
I watch from the sidelines as girls talk head on shoulder
There, like an unwanted stranger.
From as young as 5 until today
This feeling of rejection has followed me
No matter how confident I think I am
 belonging…
I know I have felt it
When my classmate sat next to me and we talked
   the whole ride
When I hold a baby.
Nestled up to my mother
My head on her chest
Going up, and down.
My hands are cold so she rubs them
I am afraid and she comforts me.
That is home to me.
But she is gone
And yet I still feel that as I think of her.
When I am with my brothers

Laughing about things nobody else

Perhaps all our lives are falling apart yet somehow we are still
    together.

None of these people can take away the rejection from my
    peers.

Nothing will replace the home I had with my mother.

Yet, they remind me that belonging and home

Are not impossible to feel.

So perhaps creating a home does not mean—

Rely on yourself.

Perhaps it means,

Appreciate that you have a sense of home

Even if it doesn't look like what others have.

Maybe belonging within yourself means—

finding belonging wherever you go.

Knowing it is not limited to the ways

    those around you are belonging.

I feel rejection, insecurity, loneliness

I feel warmth, home, belonging

What will I focus on?

I was fine for so long

I was fine for so long
and suddenly I'm having thoughts I'm afraid of
the thoughts I pushed down for so long
and suddenly my world feels so rocked
yet I have learned that I have to let these thoughts come
and let them go
and let them make me feel however they make me feel
and know it will all be ok
that these thoughts won't hurt me
and they are part of who I am
it's ok to question
and to wonder what I'm doing here
and to wonder what the point of everything is if Moshiach
    isn't here yet
and will it come and if it isn't real then is nothing real?
and through this dark dark exile
we will emerge victorious
and there's a part of me that can never stop believing
even if I want to
and sometimes I wish I could stop believing,
because this world is so confusing with it,
but more confusing without it
there has to be a purpose

because I believe that if there wasn't one,

then we wouldn't feel like we needed one.

I don't know exactly why I'm here

I don't know what the future holds,

I cannot be certain of anything.

Those words used to be uttered with trembling lips
    and shaking hands

and now those words are uttered with a certain comfort.

because there are those smarter and older then me who believe

there are those before, and before, and before who believe.

and when I cannot rely on my own faith,

I rely on the faith of those who came before me.

of those who had the same questions

and still held steadfast

and still believed

and I rely on the strength within

the part of me that persevered through all those panicked
    moments and still,

I prayed.

I prayed to an invisible G-d

that I somehow knew existed

and now when I question why am I am here

I remind myself what an important question that is
and how it can move me forward

I may not have all the answers
and I know only what I can know,
so I work with the knowledge that I have
and the belief in the knowledge that I don't have.

If G-d were to speak to me
I imagine perhaps this is what He would say

My dearest child

You are like to me as an only child born to an elderly couple.

My only,

My precious.

My love,

It Is unlike any love you can possibly feel,

It is unlimited!

I know sometimes you look for me

 you wonder where I am

You wonder why I did what I did

You wonder why I made you the way I made you.

And sometimes I see you forget about me

You try to deny me

You wish you can hate Me for all the "bad"

   and pain I have caused you.

My child,

You do not see what I see,

You do not see the potential in everything

   to reveal its true goodness.

But that is exactly why I put you here.

To wrestle with the bad I have given you

To subdue it so as to reveal its true essence.

Know my child that I created the struggle

I created the part within you that you feel will destroy you.

But I did not create it to destroy you

I created it to build you.

And know my child you do not fight this war alone.

I put a spark of Me within you.

That is the part that can't ever be touched or hurt
  no matter what you do.

But that is not the only part I love about you.

I love you in your entirety

Every part of you.

And now You look at me

Try to find me

Try to understand How you can trust me.

I know you feel I have let you down.

But my dearest,

My love,

I did not let you down

I raised you up.

You worry for your future

What will be?
Who will take care of me?
And you look at me and say G-d!
"How can I trust you?
How can I know I will be ok"?
You don't know my dear
But I do
I know exactly what will be for you.
I am holding you and guiding you,
I am sending you what you need.
And when you feel that I am letting you down
Remember this,
I am raising you up.
I am bringing you close

And I will never ever let go.

Epilogue

Looking Towards the Future

My high school graduation speech, June 2022,
B'nos Chomesh Academy, Brookly, NY

I have heard of graduating being compared to being, at the edge of a cliff. You are afraid to fall. On my graduation trip my class and I hiked to the edge of a cliff. I was not only afraid. I was amazed. It was beautiful up there. However, I can't see my future from a high view, I feel like I am falling down the cliff, not just looking at its beautiful scenery.

After my mothers passing when I was 13 I felt like I was falling down a cliff. I didn't see a beautiful future, I felt insecure.

I am afraid.

And for years I believed that was the only feeling I could have about the future. And slowly I started to see hope and excitement. Slowly I started to realize that my life is not defined by what I have been through. That I can change the habits and break free of the bonds holding me back.

This year I have learned many things but one of the most important things I have learned is what it really means to trust in Hashem. That just as I am here now He will guide me to my next step. He will put me in exactly the right spot just as the stars are in their proper place to shine light in a way only they could. I am where G-d put me to shine my light.

Looking towards the future I see light,and joy,Growth, and connection. I see how my learning will never end.

I see all this from the view that BCA gave me. Bca gave me the space to see a life beyond my mother's death. By showing me that there is always hope and change and things can get better. By allowing space for my grief. I live with my mother. She is on my journey and part of who I am. So I am opening this space for her. It is so much easier for me to hide away and forget about her. But on this day I feel I cannot let her be pushed aside no matter how painful. As I acknowledge all that BCA has done for me, as I acknowledge my accomplishments from this year I cannot forget to acknowledge that behind this success is my mother. Her love, pride, belief in me is everlasting, even though it's hard for me to feel.

I have been climbing this mountain of high school for four years. I have been climbing this mountain called grief for almost six and now, I am standing on this mountain of

Belief in my self, Belief in the goodness of those around me, Belief in G-d.

And I believe all this because BCA did not just say these thing but they showed me—What I can be.

They trusted me. And so looking towards the future, I am afraid

But I also believe there is so much more to this beautiful world then my fear. There is trust, and with trust comes serenity and joy, and beauty at every stage.

It may be a long steep climb, but I am learning to enjoy the hike.

Chassidus Essay

I lost my mother at the young age of 13. It was like a wall had fallen on me. A mother is one of the most powerful relationships a person can have. Her child looks to her mother as her protector. I have wondered how I can ever feel secure when the one who you always turned to is gone?

I feel as if I am left alone and unheard. If I fall, there is nobody to catch me.

G-d is the Father of orphans and it is said that He listens to the cries of orphans. People have told me that I am G-ds first priority. How can I feel that if I don't see it, if when I cry out but nobody can answer me? how could you tell me that G-d really cares?

How can I connect to an infinite, omnipotent being in the way I would feel a connection with a parent?

The Baal Shem Tov[1], the founder of chassidus, lost both of his parents by the time he was five years old. "The last words spoken to me by my holy father before his passing were: "Yisrolik, fear nothing but G-d alone." Consonant with my father's words I was drawn to walk the fields and the great, deep forest near our village."

It is interesting that spending time in nature was the way young Yisroel knew not to fear anything but G-d. He had trust that even in a forest where there may be wild animals or it may be hard to find food to sustain himself G-d would protect him. He had nothing to fear. It is Hashem's world and it's beautiful and perfectly orchestrated. Look at one branch of a tree, or

---

[1] https://www.chabad.org/library/article_cdo/aid/2529/jewish/Baal-Shem-Tovs-16th-Birthday.htm

the constellations of the stars. There is an entire world even on one small blade of grass. If G-d cares for every single atom and molecule even more so he cares for me!

One way to make this more practical to our lives is to notice the little things that went right today. Of course the things that went wrong are also G-d but for the purpose of this lets focus on the good. In any way, small or big, how did G-d take care of me today? He restored my soul to me this morning. My body works. I can see and hear and smell and taste. Noticing that G-d is sustaining me at this moment I can feel His love for me. This is another way to recognize how I am not alone.

I know G-d is with me but I want my mother!

To quote a letter from the Rebbe, "The soul is enduring and eternal, and sees and observes what is taking place with those connected with her and close to her." It is hard to connect to someone who has passed away. You can no longer see them, hear them or feel their comforting arms around you. They are beyond the world and a soul connection is so hard to feel.

Music is the pen of the soul, and so to internalize this feeling a nigun comes to mind.

Nigun hishtatchus was composed by the Tzemach Tzedek, the third Lubavitcher Rebbe. I first heard of it when I was in camp in the seventh grade just about a month after my mother's passing. The story of this nigun is a sad one. Devorah Leah[2], the daughter of the Alter Rebbe, sacrificed her very

---

[2] One day the Alter Rebbe called in his daughter Devorah Leah and told her a metaphor of a tree. A tree yields fruit and is health and whole but after 70 years it dies. He was telling her that chassidus was in danger, something was going to happen to her father. So she made a promise that whatever would happen to her father would happen to her instead.

life so that her father could live and spread chassidus. The
Tzemach Tzedek was her son. He went through the loss of
his mother at the very raw age of three. He would sing nigun
Hishtatchus at her kever. The nigun is a slow, introspective
tune." Nigun Histatchus" is a melancholic song, filled with
longing, with a palpable void of deep—felt loss. It speaks softly
and slowly, painfully expressing a deep sadness. And yet, it
doesn't fall apart, nor sink into despair. It is deliberate, weighty
and measured, unwavering with stamina and strength."

The nigun is a conversation, a question from a child to his
parent who no longer is with him. Why? He asks, why did you
leave me?

And so Devorah Leah answers him, "My child, I had to
sacrifice my life. It was for Chassidus."

And so he answers, "I understand but I still want you, I know
you are with me, but I still miss you."

And so the conversation continues, as the song goes from the
stanza to stanza. It is a song which never ends. No matter how
many answers a person can be given, the question will remain.
It is more than a question, it is a yearning. A yearning which
cannot ever be satisfied.

This song has been my anthem, it has taught me that though
I may always feel this void, I shall not crumble. The approach
of Chabad Chassidus is one of joy, but one cannot attain this
joy before they have fully journeyed through the grief. One
cannot feel truly connected until they have felt the yearning
for connection. The Tzemach Tzedek has another song,
known as "Yemin Hashem." It is an upbeat, joyous song, one
that expresses real joy and true faith. The translation is, " The
right hand of the Lord is exalted; the right hand of the Lord
performs deeds of valor." [3]

Through the darkness we can rise higher, we can attain greater trust in G-d. Trust that he will be there for us and deliver us. Faith that he really does care and look out for us.

Through the yearning I can feel a deep sense of connection. A connection with my mother. A oneness with G-d.

³ https://www.chabad.org/library/article_cdo/aid/3297601/jewish/
Exuberant—Song—Haunting—Melody.htm